Money Tips

from the

Budget Bitch

The Book of Don'ts

Carmel McCartin

Money Tips from the Budget Bitch
The Book of Don't's.

First published in 2007 by Budget Bitch Pty Ltd

This edition published 2013 by Budget Bitch Australia

Formatting: Michael Betts

Published by Budget Bitch Pty Ltd
ABN 65 123 977 480

Kingston Road Thurgoona NSW 2640

www.budgetbitch.com.au

ISBN: 978 9875113 1 7

1. Don't spend more than you earn.

This would have to be so obvious, that it's almost ridiculous. Sadly though, many people *do* spend more than they earn, on a consistent basis.

This is the basic cause of too much debt. Most people do not even realise that they're spending more than they earn. Do you have a credit card that you cannot pay out in full when the statement arrives? Do you have bills sitting on the fridge waiting to be paid? If you do - then you are spending more than you earn.

1. Do save a little each week.

No matter how small an amount you save each week, this money will eventually grow into substantial savings for your future.

2. **Don't buy things 'on sale' just for the sake of it**.

Just because something is being sold as a sale item doesn't mean that it is at a cheaper price than it was a couple of weeks ago. And the chances are - you don't even need that sale item. Check the everyday prices before you head for the sales.

2. Do your homework before you buy.

Shopping around for the best price or the best deal will save you money.

3. **Don't go to the supermarket without a shopping list**.

    It's just crazy to think you can remember everything you *need* to buy when you do the grocery shopping. This is the biggest place that 'impulse buying' happens. Look at the way the supermarket is designed. Are the everyday things on your list at the front of the store? Even if you went to the supermarket everyday, you would still buy something that you didn't need, unless you have a list of items to buy.

3. Do make a list before you leave home.

Make sure you only buy what you need. That way you won't succumb to marketing ploys and impulse buying.

4. Don't think you can over–spend now and make it up later.

This never happens because there is always *something* that will require you to spend your money as well. So many times we find that we have spent more than we had intended and it's so easy to just allow the balance to mount up on the credit card or a personal loan. Of course we always have good intentions of paying it back as soon as possible but, sadly; this is something that rarely happens.

4. Do have a plan in place to make sure you always have something in your savings account to cover the extra-ordinary expenses.

5. Don't think you can fill the limit on your credit card and not have to pay it back.

Most of us forget that the money owing on the credit card is just that – *owed money!* You are *borrowing* money every time you use that credit card. If you don't pay it back as soon as possible, you will have to pay *more* money just for the privilege of borrowing that money in the first place.

5. Do be aware of the interest charges plus the fees on your credit cards and allow for this in your budget plan.

6. Don't put a budget plan off till tomorrow.

We all know that "tomorrow never comes". You can't start a budget, if you haven't got a plan! This is the first step in taking control of your money. Why not just plan it today…. And start it right now!

6. Do sit down and prepare a budget.

The benefits of doing this will outweigh the headache and heartache of discovering just *what* sort of state your finances are in.

7. Don't buy things "just in case".

I know so many people who do this. They buy extra food, extra soap, extra detergent, and extra pantyhose. The list is endless and they always tell me that they "bought it just in case".

So, I ask - Just in case what? Is there going to be another world war that we haven't heard about? Is rationing about to be re-introduced? Are all the supermarkets going to close down? Or is it just in case we have an empty cupboard that we don't know what to put in it?

Look in your cupboard... does "just in case" mean that you have almost a case full of that item?

7. **Do have some emergency supplies of the essentials.**

Make sure that 'emergency' doesn't mean 'over-abundance'.

8. Don't go shopping to cheer yourself up when you're feeling miserable.

Yes, I know... all the self-help books tell you to "buy yourself something nice" when you're feeling down in the dumps. Well goodness me - there must be thousands of people out there feeling miserable every day. How much more miserable will you feel when you see the credit card statement at the end of the month?

You *don't* have to go shopping. There are plenty of other things you can do. Try taking a walk, riding a bike, flying a kite. Perhaps you could try reading a book, doing some gardening, or maybe even just talking to somebody.

"Getting out of the house" doesn't mean you have to go shopping.

8. Make a list of all the things you would like to *do*, rather than all the things you would like to *buy*.

9. Don't waste your money.

We waste so much of other things that it seems as if money should be one of them also. What do we waste? You ask?

Well, we waste time, and we waste effort. We waste food (just how much *does* go into the rubbish bin?) and we waste water. We waste lawn clippings and compost. Fuel is wasted when we drive needlessly. The list is endless.

Because we waste so many other things, we also waste our money.

Think about how much of everything that you can save and you'll find that you can save money too.

9. Do make a 'waste log' for a week.

Put everything into this log, not just money. By doing this you will have a real idea of exactly where you can cut back and recycle. You'll be surprised by the results.

10. Don't take your ATM card when you go out for a gamble.

If you *do* feel you can afford to gamble with your money (and let's face it - it's *your money, and your life*, and *you* make the choices to spend them how you wish), then only have the money you're prepared to spend in your wallet.

Be prepared to come home with nothing.

10. Do face the reality of how much you spend when you feel like a "flutter".

Many times the money mounts up to a greater figure than you realise. So *do* ask yourself the reason you've spent that money.

11. Don't use window-shopping as a regular form of entertainment.

This will leave you feeling dissatisfied with your life and all that you have. You will begin to 'want more than you can afford'. Sure, it might not cost anything to window-shop at this point in time, but the long-term costs can be horrendous.

There are many other forms of entertainment that cost the same in the short term but which have much more positive long- term benefits.

11. **Do look in the windows at Christmas time**.

Many of the stores make a lot of effort to impart good cheer with their displays. Pay particular attention to the displays that are designed to entertain rather than advertise.

12. Don't leave your Christmas shopping till the last minute.

There are so many of us that do this... and then we find that because we're out of time, we dash about in a frenzy and actually spend more than we intended. Sometimes we even buy things that are totally unsuitable, either as gifts or refreshments.

How many times have you finished the festive season with almost half the foodstuffs that you started with? Sure, it means you may not have to shop for a week or two but are mince pies, nuts and pretzels really something you want to eat everyday?

A little pre-Christmas planning and thought will go a long way in making sure your budget parameters are met.

12. Do make lists well before December.

Buy gifts to suit the tastes of a particular person rather than buying a gift to suit a monetary figure.

13. Don't forget to put a little aside for your future.

A little bit, often, is a good way to start saving for your future. It doesn't have to be more than a few cents every day, or even a couple of dollars every week. It's a good habit to have. Before long you'll actually be able to see your savings grow.

13. **Do investigate the different savings accounts available.**

Some of these pay a reasonable amount of interest. If there are no fees on the account, you'll find your money growing quicker.

14. Don't be afraid to say no.

Many of us grew up when money *seemed* to be in short supply. In actual fact, our parents only bought things that they had the 'cash' for. Not a bad idea, but it always seemed (at the time) as if they were saying "no".

Obviously, we felt a bit dejected that we couldn't have everything that *we'd* have liked. However we were clothed, educated and fed. Generally, it was a happy time in our lives. Naturally we all want the best for *our* children and we don't want to deny them anything, but it *is* OK to say NO.

After all, *we* didn't grow up to be such deprived people, did we?

14. Do stand in front of the mirror every day and repeat "I'm sorry; we can't afford it right now".

Say these words 10 times every day until you're comfortable that you can say 'no' without feeling guilty. It's ok to have a giggle when you're doing this.

15. **Don't try to "keep up with the Jones family",** particularly if your name isn't Jones.

We all like to 'mirror' our friends (and we do that without even thinking about it), but if *they* have something that you cannot afford – then don't go and buy one also. And don't borrow the money for it… even if it's something that you think you *really* want.

If you really can't afford it - borrow theirs!

15. Understand that our friends like us for who we are - not for what we have.

16. Don't pay your bills early.

At the same time, don't pay them late either. Let the bill money sit in your account, where it may earn you a little interest, until the time when the bill is due.

16. **Do have a system in place to make sure your bills are paid on time, every time.**

A budget will make this easier to achieve.

17. Don't be afraid of second hand places.

There are so many things you can buy secondhand - clothing, furniture, white goods, electrical goods, cars, even houses. And there are so many places you can buy them – shops, private sellers, even on the internet. Just because they've had previous owners doesn't mean they're no good.

How often have you bought something, used it once, then given it away? Or how often have you had a garage sale to get rid of your surplus goods? Charities appreciate people like you. You've probably told those charities "there's nothing wrong with it, it's just like new".

So… if you're prepared to give away things you've only used *once*, don't be ashamed to go to a secondhand place to *buy* something that you're only going to use once. You'll save a lot of money.

17. **If you really *are* worried about what your friends might think - take them with you and discover the delights of a shopping expedition which won't cost the earth.** You'll probably even have money left over for a coffee.

18. Don't buy take-away if you have a pantry full of food.

OK… go and have a look in your pantry. Is there food in there? If there is - why did you just go and buy take-away? And if you have take-away or eat out a lot - then why do you have food in your pantry? It just doesn't make sense!

What is the food in the pantry for?

18. Plan a weekly menu.

Put it in a place where you can refer to it often. Include the days you will be eating out, or would like take- away food.

19. Don't buy a season ticket to the opera if you don't like opera.

I know this tip sounds "too obvious" but how many times have you bought something, e.g.; a set of golf clubs, a bike, a membership to the gym, and *never used it?* Often you've had good intentions, and have thought you might have used it, but there it is - laying on a shelf somewhere, gathering dust.

Unless you *know* you will use it regularly - don't buy it.

19. Do try to organize a 'try before you buy' arrangement.

This way you will have a better idea if the expense will be good value and will save frittering away your hard earned cash on a whim.

20. Don't ring your neighbour if they're at home.

With telephone calls becoming cheaper, it's so easy to become complacent about the cost of communicating with your neighbours. Just ask yourself – how many times in a month have you called somebody that you could have spoken to in person?

Go visit them instead! You don't have to stay long and both of you will feel the benefit of a face-to-face encounter.

20. Do think about the use of your phone and cut back the calls.

21. Don't buy a plasma television if you have to borrow the money.

You've probably already got a good television - and yes - I know - you'd just love one of those "up-to-the-minute" technological wonders. But really - unless you have the money to pay for it now, it's just not worth borrowing the money to have it.

In the long run, you'll be paying more for the screen (because it is borrowed money) and by the time you've actually *saved* for it - you'll find the prices have come down anyway.

21. **Put some money aside each week and save the price of the television.**

By the time you have saved enough to pay cash   you will be in a better position to negotiate a better deal.

22. Don't be afraid to ask for a discount.

If you have the money to pay for something on the spot - why wouldn't you ask for a discount? Have you ever thought about it? So many people pay with credit that it must be a welcome change to have a customer with cash.

With 'merchant fees' and bank charges mounting for the retailer these days, there must at least be some room to discount the price if you want to pay cash.

What's the worst thing they could say to you? No?

22. Practice *these* words in front of a mirror each day... "What's your best price, if I pay cash?"

23. Don't replace it, if it's not broken.

Yeah, I know… sometimes we get tired of the same old things everyday. And of course - we've all heard that old saying - "a change is as good as a holiday". We probably *did* love that crockery or those rugs when we bought them. And maybe the television isn't 'state of the art' in technology ….

So why are we replacing them? What are we going to do with the old stuff? Is this the only way we know to 'spark up' a dull life?

23. A new attitude can be just as refreshing as new possessions!

24. Don't buy flowers if you have a garden.

There is nothing nicer than fresh flowers to bring cheer to a dreary room and to brighten our lives. At the risk of having every flower vendor screaming at me - it's expensive to send flowers to somebody. It doesn't cost a lot of money to grow them, and most flowers require little attention in the garden or a pot.

Pick them for yourself as a reward, or pick them for somebody as a gift. Flowers from your garden will last much longer than commercially grown flowers, and the pleasure will be much greater.

24. If you look after your garden and your savings in the same fashion both of them will soon be blossoming.

25. Don't fight about money.

Sadly, most fights start with money - the lack of it, the cost of things, one person wanting more, another spending more …. and on it goes.

Think about the last argument you had. At the core of the argument, was there a money issue involved? Aim to improve your life by *not* arguing about money.

There are other things you can fight about, if you really *are* looking for a 'barney'.

25. **The most commonly used form of an anti-depressant cure is 'shopping'.** Unfortunately, it's not the cheapest way to make you feel better.

26. Don't throw out the bath water if it's still hot.

Oh, the luxury of wallowing in a steamy hot bath after a long day! There is nothing quite like it. But it costs money to heat the water and run that bath.

Maybe there is somebody else in the house that might like to have a soak also? If there isn't, then maybe there is something you could wash in the water? Curtains perhaps? Jumpers? Rugs? The dog? Or maybe you could wash the car with it. (You only need 2 buckets of water and a sponge to wash an average car).

When the water is cold - consider watering the lawn or the plants, with whatever is left.

26. Do **investigate ways of using your 'grey water'**. Water is the most precious commodity we have.

27. Don't throw plastic bags away.

There are so many uses for plastic bags but because there are so many plastic bags available, we've forgotten that they can be recycled. That's the best thing about a plastic bag - you can always use it again.

Have you ever thought of washing the sandwich bags (on a weekly basis)? Or maybe using the supermarket plastic bags as waste bin liners?

Apart from saving the environment, you'll also save yourself some small change that you can use for other things.

27. **Do try to save some money by using each plastic bag for a minimum of 3 times.** Make it a game and see how many uses you can find for each bag.

28. Don't fill the kettle if you only want one cup of tea.

I have a friend who *never* boils the kettle for just one cup of coffee. Instead, she fills the kettle every morning and pours the boiling water into a thermos.

I used to think she was nuts, until she explained the statistics about the cost of electricity to boil the kettle, plus the environmental damage in using that electricity or gas, as well as the wasted water from the steam etc, etc, etc. She uses the hot water from the thermos to make her coffee throughout the day. She drinks a lot of coffee. She has a healthy bank balance.

Maybe she's not as nutty as I thought.

28. Watch your usage of utilities. While they *are* essentials, there are still savings to be made.

29. Don't buy a gift if you could make something just as nice.

How many times have we heard "it's the thought that counts"? Well, guess what? *That really is true.*

Think about the last time your child made you a card, or your husband picked you a flower from the garden, or your friend made you a cake. Didn't you really appreciate the thought? Of course you did!

So next time you want to give a gift, think about what that person would truly love. More than likely it won't be something from a store. They'd probably just love somebody to mow their lawns for them, or bake them a cake. Maybe they'd love you to mind their kids while they had a night out. Perhaps you could paint their spare room.

Sometimes giving *your* time is more valuable than anything you purchase.

29. Do tell them that you love them - it's more valuable than a store bought gift.

30. Don't buy an annual rail ticket if you drive to work regularly.

Yes it's true! You *can* save a lot of money by using public transport and buying an annual ticket. But if you do that - then use it!

Keep the car at home even on rainy days. It's cheaper to invest in a good umbrella than to pay for petrol, and parking fees.

30. A car-pool will also save you money.

31. Don't complain if you don't know where your money has gone.

You're the only person who hands over *your* money! Sometimes we're so busy paying bills and buying things that we lose track of where all the money has gone. By the end of the month our finances are out of control.

Be mindful of how much you are spending, where it's going and how often. *You* have control of your money - the least you can do is know where it's gone.

31. Do keep a diary of what you spend every week.

32. Don't hoard.

Oh dear! Every family has at least *one* hoarder! I come from a family where there are lots! I even have a brother-in-law who literally has *sheds* full of stuff. He calls it his "CCIH" file. (Could Come In Handy). Some of the stuff is new, some of it is waiting to be recycled and the ultimate waste of money is when he buys something new that he already has in a shed!

People who hoard things have no idea how much money is sitting in a box, or a cupboard, or a shed. Chances are - they will *never* use whatever is sitting in there! They probably don't even know what they have any more!

Ask yourself why you do this? If it's because you have too many empty cupboards and you feel a need to fill them, then maybe you need to get rid of the cupboards! Maybe you really don't need such a big house if you have to fill it with things that you will never use.

Be ruthless! Get rid of the hoard and reduce your clutter. Have a garage sale and make some money. You probably won't be reimbursed the full amount of what you've spent for the stuff, but it might make you think about how much money you've had sitting idle on the shelves. Ask yourself - "Am I going to use this in the next month? Have I used this or even *looked* at this in the past 12 months?"

You know what to do!

32. Do yourself a favour – clean out your cupboards and have a garage sale.

33. Don't be scared to negotiate.

This is a bit like asking for a discount and if you don't do it - then you'll never know what money you could have saved.

Sometimes if you can't get a discount on the price of something you may be able to negotiate an extra service or warranty for the cost of what you're paying.

Be brave! Be bold and negotiate a better deal for YOU!

33. **Do go to the library and borrow a book on negotiating.** There are many good books with hints and tips on how to negotiate.

34. Don't forget to reward yourself.

So you've got your budget under control and things are looking better than they ever have in the past. Now it's time to give yourself a reward! If you don't do this you'll begin to hate the new money habits that you now have, and you're in danger of falling back to your old ways.

It doesn't have to cost a lot of money to have a reward – a night out at the movies with the family or maybe a picnic to a special place with some extra treats. Perhaps you would like a simple trip to the ice-cream parlor.

Small luxuries often will help to keep things in perspective.

34. Do remember that you are doing your best.

35. Don't forget to do your homework before you sign the paperwork for a loan.

When you *are* borrowing money and the paperwork for the loan arrives - make sure you read it through, thoroughly.

Too many times we are so eager to 'get it all started' that we forget to read the fine print. There are many conditions and rules in that contract, and you might end up with a nasty surprise later.

To say you "didn't know' is no excuse. The paperwork has explained it all but you just didn't read it!

You need to know *everything* about the conditions for borrowing that money.

35. Do seek independent advice before committing to something you are not sure of.

36. Don't worry about missing a sale.

There will always be another sale. How many times have you seen the sign - "never to be repeated sale"? You know this is not always the truth because you have seen that sign every time they have a sale.

Every week there seems to be a sale of discounted goods somewhere. If you *really* watch the advertising catalogues you'll find that the same items appear on a rotational basis. And yes - the item you wanted will usually be 'on sale' again, another time.

36. Be aware of the times when regular sales are held – just don't make them a priority in your entertainment calendar.

37. Don't buy a puppy if you don't want a dog.

How cute and adorable is that puppy you've just seen? Wouldn't you love to just take it home? Of course you would! Of course you can!

Pets are a wonderful part of our lives. Just like kids, puppies grow up too. And, just like kids, they cost money.

As well as the food that your dog will eat, there are also things like: injections, veterinary bills and registration fees. There is also the bed that they sleep on, toys to play with, accessories such as collars and walking leads, grooming brushes and special shampoo to deter fleas.

Don't forget the puppy training school and obedience classes, and if you want to go away on holidays - you might have to pay accommodation costs for your pooch at a dog resort. (They like holidays too).

Apart from the cost of purchasing your pet, be prepared to make provision in your budget for them. Even *my* dog, which is *very* low-maintenance, costs me one dollar every day.

37. **While your friends are on holidays, baby-sit their pet for them.** Offer to pay all the expenses involved as this will also give you a well-rounded idea of the cost of having a pet.

38. Don't put money in the parking meter if there's a free car-park down the road.

To save time and energy, we always try to park the car as close to our destination as possible. Quite often, that means we have to *pay* for the parking spot.

But there are free parking spaces available and often they're not too far away. Look for those places and walk a little way – not only will you save some money but you'll also reap the benefits of some exercise!

38. Walking doesn't spend anything but energy.

39. Don't forget to be diligent in tracking your money.

Most people have absolutely no idea where their money goes each week. It's almost as if it disappears into a black hole, never to be seen again. If you want to change your financial future, it's essential that you keep account of exactly where your money goes.

Where you spend your money is your decision, and nobody can really tell you what to spend it on. It's *your* money but you should at least know where it has gone.

Once you have made the decision to change your spending habits it is imperative that you keep track of where *all* your money is spent. You can do this on a monthly or weekly basis, but a little bit every day will keep you aware of what position your finances are in.

39. Just do it! What have you got to lose?

40. Don't underestimate the coins in a money-box.

Before I was married, I used to put all my gold coins into a tin. At the time, I didn't know what I was 'saving for' - but the coins made my pockets heavy and I didn't miss them from my purse.

Getting married can be an expensive business. I needed as much cash as I could get. Two months before the wedding, I counted the money in the tin - $3,000!

That money paid for my dress, the flowers, the music and gifts for my bridesmaids. There was even a little left over. That was 20 years ago, but it's all relative - things cost less back then but we also earned less. What could have been a financially stressful time became much easier because of a simple habit.

40. Do get a money-box or a money jar and slip that loose change into it. It's the simplest way to save.

41. Don't carry plastic cards when you can pay just as easily with cash.

It's so easy to carry only a plastic card in your wallet these days. No longer do you have to worry about not having enough money in your pocket. Using a plastic card means you won't need to be embarrassed by discovering that you're short of cash when you get to the checkout.

But it's very hard to keep track of how much you are spending with a plastic card. Unless you write down every cent immediately, by the end of the day you will no idea of exactly how much you have spent.

If you plan each shopping trip and take enough cash to cover the purchases, you will be in a much better position at the end of the day.

41. Try this for one week … calculate how much you will need for food and fuel, then have that cash in your wallet. Use the cash and *only* that cash! Have a look at your bank balance afterwards.

Be prepared to be surprised.

42. Don't just live for today - unless you have a death wish.

We often hear people say "I'm not going to worry about saving my money because I could be dead tomorrow".

That's a strange saying because they're usually still alive the next day, and the next day, and the day after that. How often have we heard people say "I could get run over by a bus tomorrow"? True, you could - but don't you think you'll need your money *more* if that happens?

Most of us have no idea when we will die, and we will probably live for many more years. We won't have to worry about our money when we're dead but we'll worry about it every day while we're alive - if we don't make some plans for the future.

To make rash statements about "living for today" is irresponsible.

42. You *will* be a part of your future!

43. Don't think you can spend more because you earn more.

Your needs don't necessarily grow because your income is greater.

More income will mean more opportunities – to get rid of your debt quicker, and to have more savings.

More savings means you have better choices – now and in the future.

43. Have a budget plan that can be reviewed regularly to accommodate increases or decreases in income.

44. Don't give up.

As soon as you give up so will your money and all the good habits you have started. I know - it's easier to fall by the wayside than to stick to your plan. It's normal to have a few hurdles that will slow you down but you can always start afresh and get back on track again.

It just takes a little determination and a good budget plan.

44. **Do be prepared for a few hiccoughs along the way**. If you accept that things won't always run to plan, then you're sure to be able to pick up the pieces and keep going.

45. Don't buy things you want - buy things you need.

Everybody wants 'what money can buy' but there are very few of us that actually have the income to be able to buy 'everything'.

Until you have a solid savings plan and a healthy savings account, the things you need are much more important than the things you want.

45. Do have a list of 'the essentials'. Ask yourself if everything on that list is a 'must have' or a 'want to have'.

46. Don't buy a 4WD if you never drive off the bitumen.

The advantages of owning a 4WD are big – more space on the inside, more space on the road, more 'presence' and they are easier to find in the parking lot. They're designed to take you to places, off-road, that you've never been before. WOW!

But if you're never going to drive *off* the bitumen - why would you buy something that costs you more to purchase, more to insure and more to put fuel into?

46. **Do be sensible about the car you drive.** Ask yourself *why* you drive that type of vehicle and whether it can be replaced with one that is less expensive to operate.

47. Don't go to the supermarket everyday - unless you work there.

It's true - if you go to the supermarket every day then your grocery bill will be much higher than if you shop for groceries once a week. If you don't believe that - then try it.

For one week - go to the supermarket every day, as you normally would. Write down what you spend after each trip. Then - for the next week, just go to the supermarket once. Make sure you buy enough food and supplies for the coming week. Now compare the two different bills!

47. Make a list and shop once a week. This will save you time *and* money.

48. Don't get into a 'shout' at the pub.

Imagine this scenario - you go to the pub and find half a dozen of your mates are drinking there. Immediately they call you over and buy you a beer. This means that you have to then buy *them* a beer, because you're now "in a shout". A few more mates join you, and the 'shout' gets bigger.

Before long your wallet is feeling the strain but you've had a few beers and you can't remember whose turn it is to buy the next one. So you 'shout' again.

A few of your mates leave, perhaps a few more join in - and you're all having a great time. You've had maybe 6 beers in a short space of time, and your shout seems to be coming around quicker and quicker. Has everybody taken a turn and paid for a round? With all the comings and goings and the amount of beer consumed, it really *is* hard to keep track of where the money is going.

Don't be afraid to just buy your own beers. If they're really your mates they will understand, and they'll still drink with you. They probably have to watch *their* money just like you. The ones that don't want to drink with you were probably the ones that didn't take their turn at shouting anyway.

If you *do* feel that you need to 'shout your mates' at the pub - just take enough cash with you to do this. Be prepared to accept the fact that some of them won't buy you a beer in return.

48. **If you are going out for a 'session' make sure you also have enough money to catch a cab home again.**

49. Don't be a bludger!

The Macquarie dictionary defines a bludger as somebody who "evades responsibility, does nothing, and imposes on others" amongst other things.

We rarely hear this word these days. Back before people lived in a 'have it now, pay for it later' lifestyle a bludger was something that people aspired NOT to be.

Sadly, today we have all sorts of people who want everything and expect others to pay for it. Financial responsibility seems to have gone out the window.

From kids who are *still* living off their parents in their twenties and thirties, to people who allow their debt levels to sky-rocket. Anti-discrimination laws forbid us to label people anymore but does that mean we should be proud of the bludgers that surround us?

49. **Be financially responsible for yourself and your family.** Have a plan in place to ensure you are always able to 'pay your own way'.

50. Don't throw this book away!

If you've finished reading this book, and you really don't know what to do with it - *please* don't throw it away! At the very least, it will possibly end up at the local tip - at the mercy of the rats. That's a horrible thought. *I* wouldn't like to end up there, and neither would this book.

So... give it to a friend or family member and ask them to pass it on to somebody else when they've finished with it.

That way, not only will a few more people get benefit from reading the tips in this book, but they'll also get to save some money by not having to buy it for themselves. Maybe they will contribute to your costs of purchasing this book.

50. **Do keep this book and read it often.** Open it from time to time - just to remind you of some of the traps you can fall into if you don't take care.

51. Don't be afraid to ask for help.

One of the hardest things in life is to admit that you "don't know how". There are all sorts of people available to help you change the way you manage your finances – whether it be on a long term or a daily basis.

By looking in the phone book or on the internet, you will find literally hundreds of professional people who are able to assist you with organizing a better financial future. Accountants, financial advisors and financial planners are listed. Financial Counselors are also ready to help if you're really at a 'crisis point'.

No matter what your situation, there is somebody who can help you. While we'd all like to think our personal situation is unique, have a chat to one of these professional people and you'll find that they have met with many others in the same financial position as you.

51. **Find yourself a good coach.** Look for somebody who will help you with some new habits, encourage you, and keep you motivated. They'll be worth their weight in gold, literally.

52. Don't think the change will happen overnight.

It's not easy to change old habits. Have you ever heard the saying - "you can't teach an old dog new tricks"? Well, that just isn't true!

You *can* learn new tricks. Many articles I've read from lifestyle coaches say that it takes 21 days to learn a new habit. That's only three weeks.

When you decide to take control of your finances and change your money habits it might take a little more than 3 weeks. Let's face it - you've probably got a whole lot of new habits to learn.

52. **Move   out   of   your   comfort   zones.**
Nothing will change if *you* don't.

53. Don't be scared of mucking it up.

So - you've started on the road to improving your financial position. Well done for taking the first steps to acting responsibly with your money!

It's not the easiest thing to do and you're going to make some mistakes. Don't let these get you down and don't throw in the towel. You're making some lifestyle changes and you can't get it right first time every time.

Be prepared to move forward from these mistakes and don't be too hard on yourself.

53. The people who never make a mistake will never learn anything new.

54. Don't make excuses.

"I don't have time."

"It's too hard."

"Nobody in this house is interested."

How often have you heard something like this? How often have you *said* something like that?

It's easy to convince yourself that you have a good reason for not having a budget. Easier than being accountable for the way you manage your money.

Stop doing it! Don't listen to that little voice in your head.

The only person that believes those stories is you!

54. Make up your mind to stop using excuses as a way out of taking responsibility for your budget. *You* know you can do it!

55. Don't wear your blinkers in the supermarket.

For years I always used the same brand of washing powder. If you had asked me why, I would have told you that it made the clothes white and bright, and I liked the smell. For me, there was only one packet that I focused on in the washing powder aisle of the supermarket.

Then one day I realized that this particular washing powder was more expensive than *lots* of others. In some cases it was twice the price! The obvious thing to do was to try some less expensive brands and save some money.

I'm amazed – the only *real* difference in the product I use nowadays is the price. My clothes are as clean as they were before and my wallet has a little more in it.

55. Do be prepared to try different brands of all the products from the supermarket.

56. Don't be an ostrich.

A good friend of mine works as a financial counselor. She sees lots of people who have been struggling with their debt levels until they have almost reached breaking point.

They *know* they've been having money worries for some time but they've tried to ignore them, and they hope they'll go away.

She tells me they're like an ostrich - they bury their head in the sand so they can't see the thing that is frightening them.

How many times have you ignored similar feelings like these? How often have *you* been an ostrich?

56. **Do talk to somebody about your fears.**
The greatest fear of all - is fear itself.

57. **Don't think this is the end… it's just the beginning.**

Do something *now* to change – it's *your* future!

About the Author

Carmel McCartin has had many life experiences from being a travel hostess and restaurant manager to a mortgage broker and budget consultant. These have provided her with a considerable insight into just how money can work better for anyone.

Money Tips – The Book of Don'ts is Carmel's first book.

She is also the Managing Director of Budget Bitch Pty Ltd, a boutique budget consultancy business. Many of her clients have been able to get their budgets in shape leading them to better financial health.

This book has been written to provide easy and straightforward tips for anyone wanting to change their money habits.

Need to know more or seek further help?

www.budgetbitch.com.au

If you enjoyed *Money Tips*, please check out a sneak preview of Carmel's next book, *1001 Budget Tips* available in 2013.

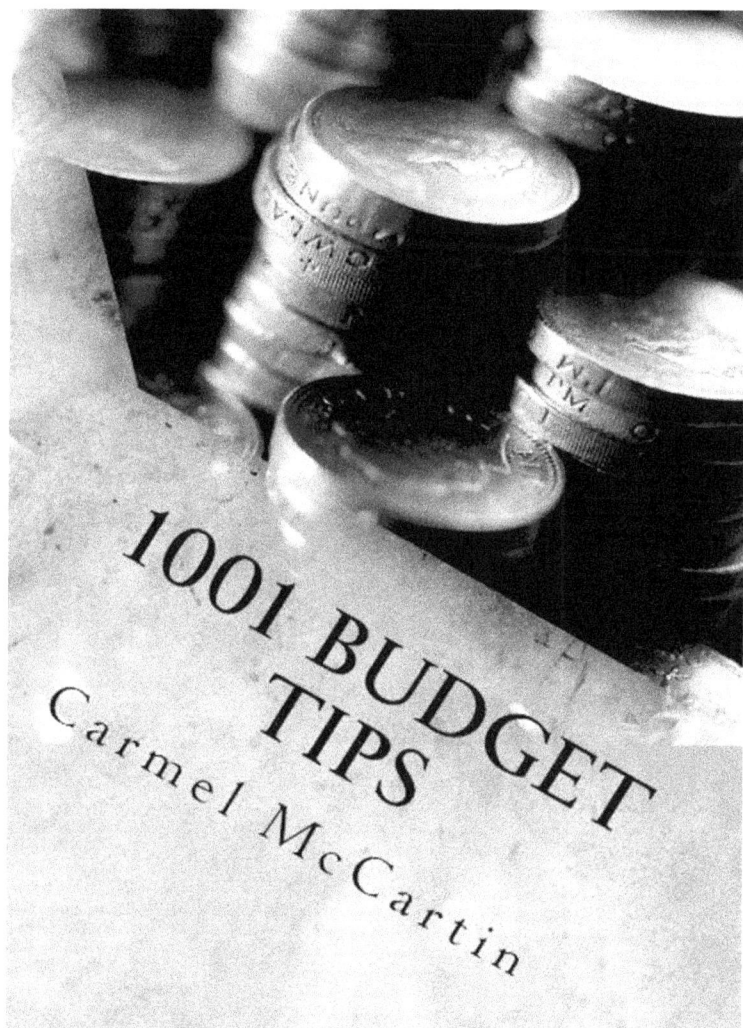

1001 BUDGET TIPS

Carmel McCartin

FOREWORD

Having a budget doesn't mean being a cheapskate. Nor does it mean you must live frugally.

It's about making the most of the money you have today.

This book holds a collection of just 1001 of my favourite Budget Tips. Some of them are old, some are new. Some of these tips have been passed down through my family, whilst others have been collected and collated from all over the world.

There are some tips that I've written for you and some that I've learned the hard way. All of them are useful.

There's no doubt that you will have heard or learned some of these Budget Tips before. Just reading them again will remind you of their worth.

It's not just a reference book though; I've included some pages for you to jot down the hints you find most memorable or the things you want to put into action immediately.

I hope you will find this book helpful in making it easier to manage your money.

Carmel McCartin

Entertainment

1. Don't use the shopping mall/centre as a form of entertainment. Window shopping will always make you dissatisfied and want to spend more money.

2. Instead of going to the cinema, save your money by staying at home and hiring a DVD instead.

3. Gym memberships average $20 a week, so unless you are a regular, it is usually not value for money.

4. Eating out two fewer times a month will save you heaps!

5. Picnics can be a great form of inexpensive entertainment - you only need a nice day, some sandwiches, drinks and maybe a ball to throw around.

6. Giving gifts from the heart, instead of the wallet can relieve a lot of stress during holidays and special occasions.

7. Go to the library to borrow your books, rather than buy them.

8. Rent toys instead of buying them - or join a toy library.

9. Check out the local museums - most of them are free and have organised children's activities during the school holidays.

10. At your local cinema, check out which day of the week is the day they have discounted tickets.

11. Get creative! Plan to make all the gifts for Christmas this year. You may need to start early if your list is large.

12. A luxuries night out does not have to be expensive. Skip the appetizer, order wine by the glass and drink more water, then share a great dessert. Keep an eye out for happy hour specials and see the latest weekend matinee.

13. Instead of hitting the spa for a full-on day, take advantage of seasonal packages or just go for a soak in the hot tub.

14. Splurge once in a while - the key to living on a small budget is to focus on your financial goals first and then splurge on your luxury items afterward.

15. Join a babysitting club - that way everybody gets to share the load at inexpensive prices. And if you can't find one - start one!

16. Have a picnic on the couch - complete with wine and cheese.

17. Look online for special offers from theme parks. Often they have a discount if you print the page and take it when you buy tickets.

18. If you belong to a large extended family, gift giving at Christmas can be costly. Consider having a 'Kris Kringle'.

19. *Read more when you buy your own copy.*

Watch for *1001 Budget Tips* available
early 2013